Changing Materials
Cooling

Chris Oxlade

www.heinemannlibrary.co.uk
Visit our website to find out more information about Heinemann Library books.

To order:
☎ Phone +44 (0) 1865 888066
▤ Fax +44 (0) 1865 314091
▣ Visit www.heinemannlibrary.co.uk

Edited by Charlotte Guillan and Catherine Veitch
Designed by Ryan Frieson and Betsy Wernert
Original illustrations © Capstone Global Library Ltd.
Illustrated by Randy Schirz (p. 8)
Illustrated by Hart McLeod (pp. 11)
Photo research by Elizabeth Alexander and Virginia Stroud-Lewis

Originated by Modern Age Repro House Ltd
Printed in China by South China Printing Company Ltd

ISBN 978 0 431 17478 5 (hardback)
13 12 11 10 09
10 9 8 7 6 5 4 3 2 1

British Library Cataloguing in Publication Data
Oxlade, Chris
Cooling. - (Changing materials)
536.5'6
A full catalogue record for this book is available from the British Library.

Acknowledgements

We would like to thank the following for permission to reproduce photographs: Alamy **pp. 7** (© Itani), **10** (© Rex Argent), **19** (© Kevin Ebi), **27** (© Bubbles Photolibrary/Ian West); Art Directors and Trip Photo Library **p. 18** (Helene Rogers); © Capstone Global Library **pp. 4 & 5** (MM Studios); © Capstone Global Library Ltd. 2004 **pp. 12 & 24** (Trevor Clifford); © Capstone Publishers **pp. 22 & 23** (Karon Dubke); Corbis **pp. 6** (© Maureen Barrymore), **16** (© Michael DeYoung), **25** (© Morgan David de Lossy); Getty Images **pp. 15** (StockFood Creative/Henrik Freek), **20** (Photonica/Roger Charity), **29** (Stone/Tom Morrison); Science Photo Library **p. 17** (Andrew Lambert Photography); Shutterstock **pp. 9** (© Nikolay Stefanov Dimitrov), **13** (© Alexander Raths), **14** (© WizData inc), **21** (© Serg64), **26** (© MaszaS), **28** (© Beata Becla).

Cover photograph of a child's hands holding ice cubes reproduced with permission of Alamy/ © Jim Wileman.

Every effort has been made to contact copyright holders of material reproduced in this book. Any omissions will be rectified in subsequent printings if notice is given to the publishers.

All the Internet addresses (URLs) given in this book were valid at the time of going to press. However, due to the dynamic nature of the Internet, some addresses may have changed, or sites may have changed or ceased to exist since publication. While the author and Publishers regret any inconvenience this may cause readers, no responsibility for any such changes can be accepted by either the author or the Publishers.

Contents

Words appearing in the text in bold, **like this**, are explained in the glossary.

About materials

How many different types of materials do you know? Can you see any wood, plastic, or metal in this photo? These are all materials we use to make things.

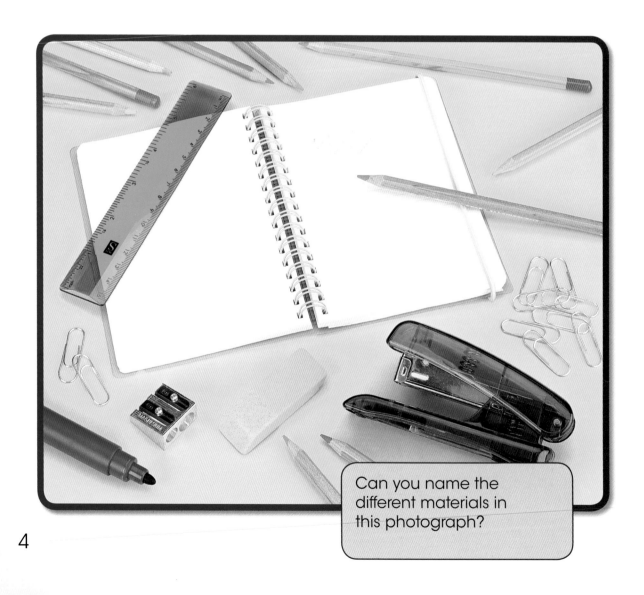

Can you name the different materials in this photograph?

Some materials are **natural** materials. We get them from the world around us. Wood, clay, and water are natural materials. Humans make other materials, such as glass and plastic.

Which of these things are made from natural materials?

Changing materials

Materials can change shape. Sometimes we can change the **properties** of a material. The properties of a material include how it looks and feels.

A sponge changes shape when you squeeze it.

Freezing food makes it go hard.

Materials often change when we cool them. Cooling a material makes it colder.

Different materials

Most materials we see are **solid** materials. But some are **liquids**, such as water. And some are **gases**, such as the air around us.

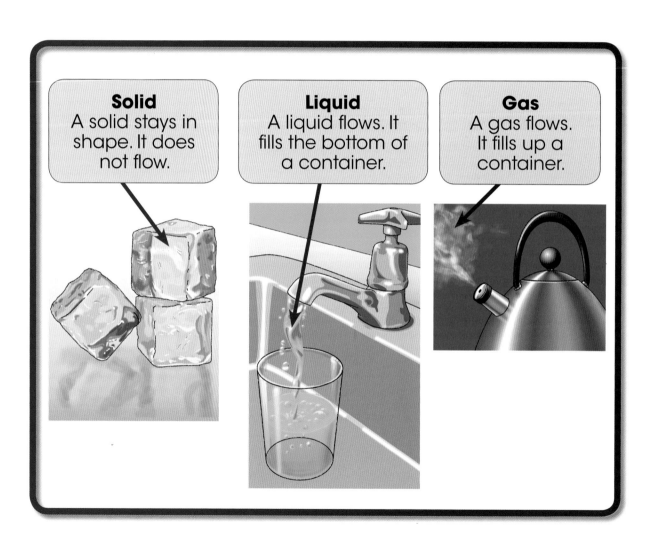

Solid
A solid stays in shape. It does not flow.

Liquid
A liquid flows. It fills the bottom of a container.

Gas
A gas flows. It fills up a container.

When a liquid material cools it can turn into a solid. When a gas cools it can turn into a liquid.

Liquid water on this window has cooled and turned into solid ice.

Hot and cold

The hot drink makes this mug feel warm.

Some things in the world around us are cold and some are hot. We can tell if things are hot or cold by feeling them. It is important to be careful because touching really hot or cold things can hurt you.

Temperature tells us how cold or how hot something is. The temperature of a cold thing is lower than the temperature of a hot thing. Temperature is measured in degrees Celsius (°C) or degrees Fahrenheit (°F).

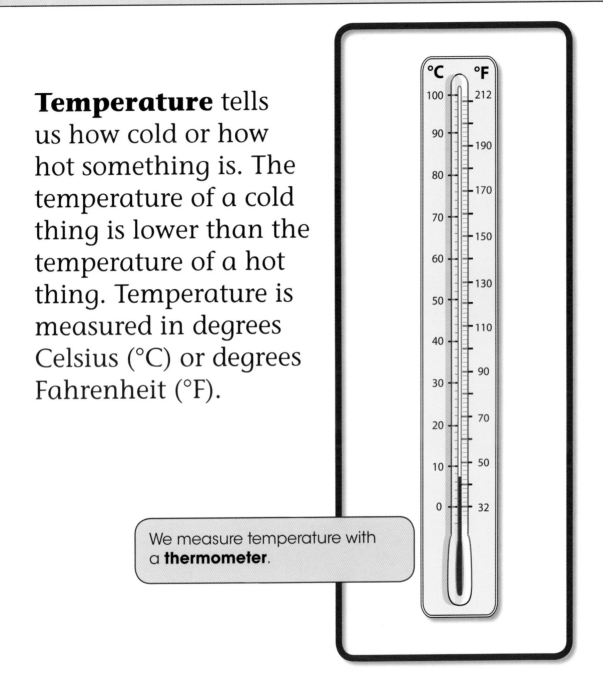

We measure temperature with a **thermometer**.

Cooling down

To cool down a material we must take heat away from it. When we take heat away, the **temperature** goes down.

The cold air in a fridge cools down the food inside.

Cooling down fish with ice keeps the fish fresh for us to eat.

There many ways of cooling things down. Ice cools things down because it is very cold. Hot things, such as hot drinks, cool down because the air around them is cooler.

Freezing

Ice forms on the top of a lake in very cold weather.

When we cool down some **liquid** materials they turn to **solids**. Water is a liquid. When it cools down it turns into ice, which is a solid.

A freezer freezes liquid.

When a liquid turns into a solid the material changes. This change is called **freezing**.

Freezing points

A material always **freezes** at the same **temperature**. For example, water always freezes at 0°C (32°F). This is called the **freezing point** of water.

Sea water freezes at about -2°C (28.5°F) because it is salty.

Antifreeze stops the water in a car's engine from freezing **solid** in cold weather.

Some materials do not freeze until they are at a temperature much lower than 0°C (32°F). Antifreeze is a special **liquid** in car engines. It does not freeze even when water does.

17

Cooling liquids

Jelly goes solid when it is cooled down.

We cool down some **liquids** to stop them being runny. For example, we put hot, freshly made jelly in the fridge to make it set. We also put soft butter in the fridge to make it hard again.

Some liquid materials are made when **solid** materials **melt**. The lava that flows from a volcano is rock that has melted deep underground. It goes solid when it cools down.

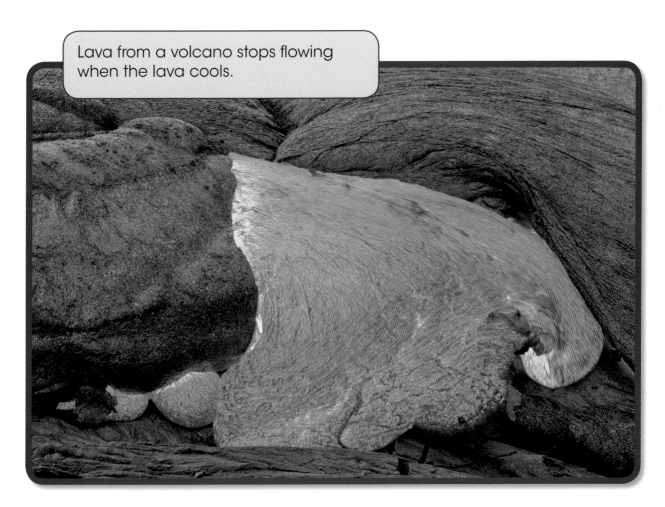

Lava from a volcano stops flowing when the lava cools.

Cooling gases

When we cool some **gases** they turn into **liquid**. **Water vapour** is water that has turned into gas. We often see water vapour turn into liquid water when it cools down.

Water vapour turns into liquid water when it touches a cold mirror.

Clouds form when the gas water vapour in the air condenses. It changes into liquid water and sometimes falls as rain.

When a gas turns into a liquid, it changes. This change is called **condensation**.

Investigating cooling

You will need a **thermometer** that measures from 0°C (32°F) to 100°C (212°F). Put some warm water into a mug. Measure the **temperature** of the water with the thermometer. Then measure it again ten minutes later.

Ask an adult to help you pour the warm water.

Empty the mug and put in some more warm water. Measure the temperature. Now add some ice to the water. Measure the temperature again ten minutes later.

The water's temperature goes down faster with ice than without it.

Making things cool

A fridge is full of cold air that takes heat away from the food.

To cool down a material, we always need something else that is cooler than the material. In the investigation on page 23, the ice was cooler than the water.

A runner can cool down with cold water.

Cold water is useful for cooling things down. Just as you can cool your face by splashing cold water over it, you can cool hot food or machines with cold water.

Stopping things from cooling

Sometimes things cool down when we do not want them to. For example, your hands cool down in cold weather. We stop things cooling by stopping the heat from escaping. Gloves stop the heat escaping from your hands.

Clothes trap heat near your body and this stops you cooling down.

Loft insulation stops heat escaping from a house roof.

In cold countries, it is important to stop homes from cooling down. People can stop the warm air escaping from their homes if they **insulate** them. This saves money on heating.

Cooling quiz

Here are some activities. Which ones do you think would cool down a hot drink? Check the answer at the bottom of page 29.

❋ Wrapping it in kitchen foil

❋ Blowing on it

❋ Putting ice in it

❋ Leaving it alone.

Be careful with hot drinks.

Here are some more activities. Which ones do you think would cool you down on a hot day?

✳ Swimming in the sea

✳ Taking a warm bath

✳ Sitting in the Sun

✳ Standing in the wind

✳ Taking off some clothes.

Would taking off a jersey cool you down? Why?

Leaving a hot drink alone is the best way to cool it down.

Swimming in the sea, or taking off some clothes are the best ways to cool down on a hot day.

Glossary

condensation when a material changes from gas to liquid

freeze when a material changes from liquid to solid

freezing point temperature at which a material always freezes

gas material that flows and fills a space. Air is a gas.

insulate cover things with material to stop them from cooling down

liquid material that flows and fills the bottom of a container. Water is a liquid.

melt when a material changes from solid to liquid

natural something that is not made by people. It comes from animals, plants, or the rocks of the Earth.

properties things that tell us what a material is like, such as how it feels and looks

solid material that stays in shape and does not flow. Wood is a solid.

temperature measure of how hot or cold something is

thermometer tool that measures temperature

water vapour gas form of water, made when water boils

Find out more

Books

Investigating Science: How Can Solids be Changed?, Jacqui Bailey (Franklin Watts, 2005)

Materials series (Cotton, Glass, Metal, Paper, Plastic, Rock, Rubber, Soil, Water, Wood, Wool), Chris Oxlade (Heinemann Library, 2002)

Temperature: Heating Up and Cooling Down, Darlene R Stille (Picture Window Books, 2004)

Ways into Science: Changing Materials, Peter Riley (Franklin Watts, 2007)

Websites

www.bbc.co.uk/schools/scienceclips

www.bbc.co.uk/schools/podsmission
There are fun materials activities on these BBC websites.

www.crickweb.co.uk/ks1science.html
Visit this website for interactive science activities.

Index